I WANT TO BE A...

POLICE OFFICER

DOUG BRADLEY

PowerKiDS press™

New York

Published in 2023 by The Rosen Publishing Group, Inc.
29 East 21st Street, New York, NY 10010

First Edition

Editor: Caitie McAneney
Book Design: Rachel Rising

Photo Credits: Cover, p. 1 VAKS-Stock Agency/Shutterstock.com; pp. 4, 6, 8, 10, 12, 14, 16, 18, 20 april70/Shutterstock.com; p. 5 John Roman Images/Shutterstock.com; p. 7 Photographee.eu/Shutterstock.com; p. 9 zef art/Shutterstock.com; p. 11 LightField Studios/Shutterstock.com; p. 13 Pixel-Shot/Shutterstock.com; p. 15 sirtravelalot/Shutterstock.com; p. 17 Steven J Hensley/Shutterstock.com; p. 19 a katz/Shutterstock.com; p. 21 Purino/Shutterstock.com.

Some of the images in this book illustrate individuals who are models. The depictions do not imply actual situations or events.

Library of Congress Cataloging-in-Publication Data
Names: Bradley, Doug.
Title: Police officer / Doug Bradley.
Description: New York : PowerKids Press, 2023. | Series: I want to be a… | Includes glossary and index.
Identifiers: ISBN 9781725339859 (pbk.) | ISBN 9781725339873 (library bound) | ISBN 9781725339866 (6pack) |
ISBN 9781725339880 (ebook)
Subjects: LCSH: Police–Juvenile literature. | Police–Vocational guidance–Juvenile literature.
Classification: LCC HV7922.B656 2023 | DDC 363.2–dc23

Manufactured in the United States of America

CPSIA Compliance Information: Batch #CSPK23. For Further Information contact Rosen Publishing, New York, New York at 1-800-237-9932.

Find us on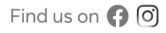

CONTENTS

What Do Police Officers Do?

Police officers are community helpers. Their job is to keep people safe. They make sure people follow the law. They can find and **arrest** people who steal from or hurt others. Some police officers work with police dogs to solve crimes!

5

Where Do Police Officers Work?

Police officers often start their workday at the police station. That's where many police officers work together. Then, they are sent out to help people when there's an **emergency**. People who break the law are sometimes brought to police stations.

It's an Emergency!

When there's an emergency, people call 911. Then, police officers go to help. Police officers help when there's a crime happening. They help when someone is hurt. They help when someone is lost. They help when there's a car crash.

In the Police Car

Many police officers drive around in a police car. Usually one or two police officers are in each car. They make sure people aren't driving too fast on the road. They also look for people breaking the law. Some police officers ride motorcycles or horses.

Keeping People Safe

Police officers are **public safety** workers. Some drive around neighborhoods to keep people from breaking the law. Some work at special events, such as parades. They make sure everyone acts fairly and no one gets hurt.

Stopping Crime

Most laws are meant to keep people safe. For example, it is unlawful to hurt someone if you aren't already in danger. It is unlawful to make or sell things that could hurt people. Police can arrest people who have broken the law.

Teaching Others

Police officers often visit schools. They also hold special events so people can meet them. They teach people about following the law. They also teach people about staying safe. They might teach kids to wear helmets on their bikes.

How to Be a Police Officer

After high school, you can go to **college** or join the **military**. Then, you go to a police academy, or school. You learn about different laws. You learn how to keep yourself and others safe. After, you learn more on the job.

Community Helper

Do you want to be a police officer? You can start by talking to police officers. Learn more about how they help your community. You can also help your community. Help older neighbors. Play by the rules. Stand up for people who need it.

GLOSSARY

arrest: To take or keep someone who is thought to have broken a law.

college: A school people can go to after high school.

emergency: An unexpected and often unsafe situation that calls for action right away.

military: Armed forces.

public safety: Having to do with keeping many people safe.

FOR MORE INFORMATION

BOOKS

Roberts, Antonia. *Police Officers*. Minneapolis, MN: Bearport Publishing, 2021.

Rossiter, Brienna. *We Need Public Safety Workers*. Lake Elmo, MN: Focus Readers, 2022.

WEBSITES

How to Use 911

kidshealth.org/en/kids/911.html#cater
Learn more about how you can call 911 if you have an emergency.

Police Dogs

www.ducksters.com/animals/policedogs.php
Explore more about a police officer's best friend—the police dog.

INDEX